SHIRE NATURAL HISTORY

of the

SARA CHURCHFIELD

CONTENTS

What is a shrew? 2
Shrews in Britain 3
Feeding habits 7
Activity and rest 15
Breeding 17
The shrew's year 18
Social organisation 21
Shrews and man 23
Useful information 24

COVER: *Common Shrew (Sorex araneus) in its burrow.*

Series editors: Jim Flegg and Chris Humphries.

Copyright © 1988 by Sara Churchfield. First published 1988.
Number 30 in the Shire Natural History series. ISBN 0 85263 951 1.
All rights reserved. No part of this publication may be reproduced or transmitted in any form or by any means, electronic or mechanical, including photocopy, recording, or any information storage and retrieval system, without permission in writing from the publishers, Shire Publications Ltd, Cromwell House, Church Street, Princes Risborough, Aylesbury, Bucks HP17 9AJ, UK.

Set in 9 point Times roman and printed in Great Britain by C. I. Thomas & Sons (Haverfordwest) Ltd, Press Buildings, Merlins Bridge, Haverfordwest, Dyfed.

What is a shrew?

The shrew is a small mouse-like mammal belonging to the family Soricidae. It is chiefly characterised by the possession of a long, pointed, mobile snout, very small eyes and short but dense dark-coloured fur resembling that of the mole. Shrews, like moles, are classed as insectivores. They also have small, rounded ears, a slender tail and short legs with five digits or toes on each foot.

The family Soricidae is large and cosmopolitan and contains a multitude of forms. Shrews are found on all the major land masses except in polar regions, the Australian region and most of South America. They also occur in a great range of climatic conditions from steamy tropical rain forests to cold tundra. There are over two hundred species of shrew, which show a variety of adaptations to different modes of life and a considerable range in size. The tiny Etruscan Shrew (*Suncus etruscus*), which weighs a mere 2 grams as an adult and has a head and body length of only 35 mm, is one of the smallest of all known mammals. It is found in southern Europe and parts of Africa and Asia. At the other end of the scale are the large, rat-sized shrews inhabiting parts of tropical Africa and Asia, the largest known being *Suncus murinus*, which can weigh as much as 106 grams with a head and body length of around 150 mm.

Most shrews live on the ground amongst dense vegetation and leaf litter. Some, however, are more specialised and are adapted to a particular lifestyle. There are mole-like, fossorial shrews which are largely subterranean and there are others which are adapted for life in desert areas. For example, the Piebald Shrew, found in parts of Soviet Asia, possesses long, stiff hairs fringing the feet which are thought to provide increased surface area and support on loose sand in the dry steppe in which it lives. It is so called because of its unusual colour pattern. While most shrews are quite uniform in colour with dark backs and pale bellies, the Piebald Shrew has a greyish-coloured back with a large white patch in the middle. The underparts, feet and tail are also white. There are even a number of semi-aquatic shrews adapted for swimming, diving and foraging underwater. These aquatic shrews, which include the European Water Shrew (*Neomys fodiens*) and the North American Water Shrew (*Sorex palustris*), also possess fringes of stiff hairs on the edges of the feet and toes which increase the surface area of the foot and so assist swimming. Some of these water shrews have been reported to run over the surface of the water for four to five seconds, evidently receiving support from the surface tension of the water and bouyancy from the air trapped by the hairs on the feet. *Chimarrogale*, an Asiatic water shrew, has particularly small ears which possess a flap of skin which acts as a valve and seals the opening of each ear when the shrew submerges, and *Nectogale elegans*, found in eastern Asia and the Himalayas, possesses webbed feet.

Some shrews possess strange features which cannot readily be explained or ascribed to a particular lifestyle since insufficient is known about their habits. The Armoured Shrew, *Scutisorex*, of central and eastern Africa has a most peculiar vertebral column. The vertebrae are unique in possessing numerous interlocking spines, creating an extraordinarily complex and sturdy structure unlike any other mammal. Such is the strength of this shrew that it is reported to be able to support the weight of a full-grown man as he steps on to the shrew and balances on one leg on its back. A shrew treated in such a way was observed to run off unharmed as soon as the man stepped off it. This shrew is also known as the Hero Shrew as it is believed to convey great powers of bravery and protection from wounds to anyone who eats parts of it or wears it as a talisman.

Shrews are almost exclusively insectivorous or carnivorous although they may supplement the diet with some plant matter. While most subsist largely on invertebrate prey, some will take much larger prey. A large part of the diet of the Piebald Shrew, for instance, comprises lizards and a captive individual was reported to have killed eleven lizards in one day, eating five of them.

Shrews are robust small mammals, resistant to cold but not to starvation, to which they succumb and die within two or three hours. Contrary to popular opinion they are not highly strung, nervous animals which die easily from shock, but when frightened their heart rate is reported to increase to an incredible twelve hundred beats per minute.

Shrews in Britain

THE SPECIES AND THEIR DISTRIBUTION

Five species of shrew are found in Britain, of which three occur on the mainland. These three are red-toothed shrews because of the deposition of iron in the outer layer of enamel of the tips of the teeth. This is thought to make the teeth harder and more resistant to wear. The species familiar to most people is the Common Shrew (*Sorex araneus*), sometimes called the shrew-mouse or ranny. The adults of this species have a dark brown pelage with pale bellies. Some individuals, around 20 per cent of the population, have distinctive tufts of white hairs on their ears and occasionally albino shrews are found. Common Shrews have a body length of 48 to 80 mm and a tail of 24 to 44 mm. The adults can weigh up to 14 grams but juveniles are somewhat smaller, weighing 5 to 7 grams, and their pelage is a lighter brown until they undergo their first moult in the autumn and grow winter coats.

The Common Shrew is distributed throughout the mainland of Britain and many of the islands but not Ireland, Shetland, Orkney, the Outer Hebrides, Scilly Isles or Channel Islands. It is known to occur on the Isle of Wight, Skomer, Anglesey, Arran, Bute, Gigha, Islay, Jura, Luing, South Shuna, Scarba, Lismore, Mull, Ulva, Colonsay, Skye,

1. *Comparative sizes of four species of shrew.*

	Body weight (g)	Head & Body length (mm)	Tail length (mm)
Water Shrew	9.0-16.0	61-72	45-77
Common Shrew	5.0-13.0	48-71	48-80
Pygmy Shrew	2.3- 5.5	40-55	32-46
Lesser White-toothed shrew	3.0- 7.0	50-75	24-44

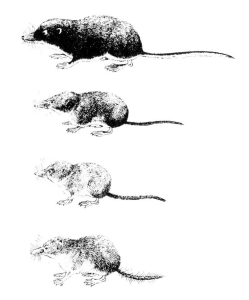

3

Crowlin and Raasay. Its presence on many of these islands is thought to be due to natural immigration from the nearby mainland. On Jersey in the Channel Islands, and in parts of continental Europe, it is replaced by a closely related and almost identical species, *Sorex coronatus*.

The Pygmy Shrew (*Sorex minutus*), as its name implies, is the smallest native British shrew. It weighs only 2.4 to 6.1 grams and has a head and body length of 40 to 60 mm and a tail length of 32 to 46 mm. It differs from the Common Shrew not only in its smaller size but in the paler brown colour of its pelage and also by its relatively longer and hairier tail. It is distributed throughout mainland Britain and occurs on all other islands larger than 10 km (6 miles) long, and also on Skomer, Lundy and many of the smaller Scottish islands. It is absent from the Scillies, the Channel Islands and Shetland. Most notably it is the only shrew found in Ireland.

The reason why the Pygmy Shrew is the only species of shrew found in Ireland is a puzzle, but it is thought to have reached Ireland by a low-lying land bridge from Scotland via Islay around eight thousand years ago, at a time when the sea level was considerably lower than it is today. Such a land bridge may have comprised wet, peaty moorland. This habitat is not much favoured by Common Shrews as they rely on earthworms for a major part of their diet and these are not abundant in acid moorland soils. Pygmy Shrews, however, do not eat earthworms, neither do they rely as much on burrow systems as do Common Shrews. It is speculated that this difference in habit could have favoured the spread of Pygmy Shrews but not Common Shrews to Ireland.

The presence of Pygmy Shrews on remote islands such as Lewis, Barra and Orkney can be explained only by accidental introduction by man, but how these minute mammals with their high metabolic rates and susceptibility to starvation could have survived the journeys is a mystery.

The largest shrew native to Britain is the Water Shrew (*Neomys fodiens*), which weighs between 12 and 18 grams and has a head and body length of 67 to 96 mm. Some Water Shrews are entirely black in colour, but in most individuals the dorsal surface is black and the belly whitish, and there are often white hairs circling the eyes and beside the ears, making this a most handsome and distinctive shrew. As its name implies, it is semi-aquatic in habit and the feet and toes are fringed with stiff hairs to assist swimming. Water Shrews are found throughout the British mainland and most of the islands, including the Isle of Wight, Anglesey and many of the Scottish islands, amongst them Skye, Mull, Islay, Arran and Hoy. It is absent from Ireland and many of the smaller islands. However, Water Shrews are not often seen as they have a localised and sporadic occurence.

The white-toothed shrews are so called because they lack the red enamel on the crowns of the teeth that is found in the other species mentioned. The two species found in the British Isles are almost identical and difficult to tell apart, and they do not occur on the British mainland. The Lesser White-toothed or Scilly Shrew (*Crocidura suaveolens*) is found on Jersey and Sark in the Channel Islands and also on all but the smallest of the Scilly Isles, including St Mary's, St Martin's, Tresco, Bryher and St Agnes. It is thought to have been introduced to the Scilly Isles by man, probably accidentally by traders from France or northern Spain as they came to the Cornish coast in search of tin in the iron age or possibly earlier. How these shrews could have survived for considerable periods of time aboard ships is not known.

The Greater White-toothed Shrew is slightly larger but otherwise very similar in outward appearance, but in the British Isles it is found only on the Channel Islands of Guernsey, Alderney and Herm, where it is thought to have been introduced by man. Both species have a much wider distribution in central and southern Europe and across into Africa and Asia. They resemble the Common Shrew in size but the pelage is paler and more reddish-brown in colour and the ears are larger and more prominent. They also have long, scattered hairs on the tail. These species are members of a

2 (above). *The Pygmy Shrew is Britain's smallest native shrew.*

3 (right). *European Water Shrew (side view).*

4. Water Shrew foraging underwater.

large and widespread group of shrews which has a southerly distribution in warm climes, and they are at the edge of their range in Britain.

HABITATS AND POPULATION DENSITIES

Shrews are ubiquitous little mammals and can be found in all terrestrial habitats. Although some species inhabit hot desert areas, shrews occur most frequently in moist habitats where there is plenty of vegetation cover and an abundance of invertebrate prey for them. They may also be found in mountainous areas amongst scree at considerable altitudes: Common Shrews have been reported at 1000 metres (3300 feet) in Britain.

Most shrews are able to climb and burrow a little but they generally live on the ground surface amongst vegetation, hiding in nests in grass tussocks or under logs. They also occupy and modify underground crevices and tunnels created by other small mammals more adept at burrowing. However, they have been found occupying nests of harvest mice in bushes.

In Britain, Common and Pygmy Shrews are found mostly in deciduous woodland, hedgerows, grassland and scrubland. They will also inhabit gardens, living in hedge bottoms and even compost heaps. Common Shrews occur in greater numbers than any of the other British shrews. Their numbers vary somewhat from one habitat to another and from one season to another but their populations reach a peak in summer, when there may be some seventy individuals per hectare (twenty-eight per acre) in grassland and deciduous woodland. Population numbers are smaller in winter with up to thirty per hectare (twelve per acre) in these habitats. Populations are smaller in other habitats. Pygmy Shrews are never as numerous as Common Shrews, even in Ireland, where they are the only species of shrew present. Population studies reveal Pygmy Shrews to be about 10 to 18 per cent of all shrew captures in most habitats. They number from about eight per hectare (three per acre) in woodland to forty per hectare (sixteen per acre) in grassland in summer, but the population decreases in winter.

Water Shrews sometimes co-exist with Common and Pygmy Shrews in these same habitats, often several kilometres from water, but they are never as numerous as the other two species in these habitats. Even in their preferred habitats, which are the grassy banks of rivers, streams, ponds and drainage ditches, they occur in very small numbers. In Britain a favourite habitat for these shrews is watercress beds but even there they seem to number only around three to six per hectare (one to two per acre). They inhabit extensive burrow systems in the banks with entrances usually above water level. The reasons for their small numbers and sporadic occurrence are not known, but the modification and destruction of their habitats through drainage and clearance practices may be contributing to their decline. In north-west Scotland they occur amongst boulders on rocky beaches.

On the European mainland the white-toothed shrews are widespread in many habitats. They inhabit even dry maquis and stone walls. They are also found around human dwellings and hence are known as house shrews. In the Channel Islands and Scilly Isles they have become adapted to island life. besides the usual habitats of grassland and scrubland they are commonly found on grassy sand dunes and even amongst rocks on the seashore. While they achieve population numbers of between seventy-seven and one hundred per hectare (thirty-one to forty per acre) in Europe, they are not very numerous on the British islands that they occupy, having densities akin to those of Pygmy Shrews. In the Scilly Isles and Jersey white-toothed shrews occur together with the ubiquitous Common Shrew.

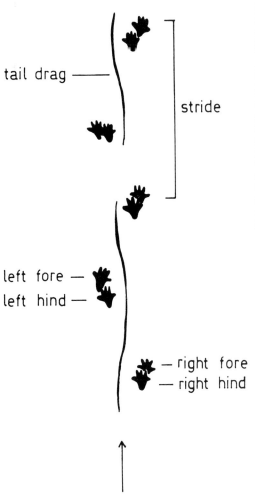

5. Trail and footprints of the Common Shrew.

Feeding habits

THE DIET OF SHREWS

Although shrews are classed as insectivores, they feed on many different types of invertebrates as well as on insects and there are few invertebrates which do not fall prey to them. Their prey ranges from tiny springtails of about 3 mm in body length to large earthworms around 60 mm long. Some species of shrew have been known to tackle even other small mammals, such as mice, and small birds, and carrion is occasionally included in their diet.

Common Shrews in Britain eat most

6 (above). *The Lesser White-toothed Shrew or Scilly Shrew.*
7 (right, above). *A Common Shrew tackling a large earthworm.*
8 (right, below). *Common Shrew grooming itself.*

terrestrial invertebrates including slugs, snails, centipedes, bugs and flies but the most important items in the diet are usually adult beetles, insect larvae, earthworms and woodlice. Pygmy Shrews have similar feeding habits but they tend to catch a higher proportion of smaller prey than Common Shrews. Their main prey are beetles, spiders, woodlice, flies and bugs. A notable difference between the feeding habits of these two shrews is that Pygmy Shrews rarely, if ever, eat earthworms in the wild, probably because they are generally too large to tackle. A positive correlation has been found between the availability of certain prey,

		WATER SHREW	COMMON SHREW	PYGMY SHREW
Terrestrial prey	Spiders			■
	Beetles	■		■
	Woodlice			■
	Bugs			
	Centipedes			
	Insect larvae			
	Slugs & snails		■	
	Earthworms		■	
Aquatic prey	Fly larvae			
	Caddis larvae	■		
	Other insect larvae			
	Crustaceans	■		

9. *The diet of shrews: an example of the relative proportions of different prey types (shown in black) eaten by shrews in Britain.*

such as beetles, and their incidence in the diet, and shrews subsist mainly on the commoner and most abundant prey types.

Water Shrews, as their name implies, are often found associated with freshwater habitats, and they feed on a range of aquatic prey, particularly freshwater shrimps and snails, water slaters, caddis larvae and fly larvae. In Britain the most important prey throughout the year are aquatic crustaceans such as freshwater shrimps, and caddis larvae. Water Shrews are also known to take much larger prey such as frogs, newts and small fish. Although they forage underwater throughout the year, regardless of the weather, aquatic prey comprise only about 50 to 60 per cent of the diet. The remainder of their diet consists of terrestrial prey, particularly beetles, spiders, molluscs and earthworms, and here they overlap in feeding habits with the Common and Pygmy Shrews. They are able to live far from water and subsist entirely on terrestrial prey.

White-toothed shrews have feeding habits which are very similar to those of Common Shrews, again with a wide variety of invertebrates being eaten. Lesser White-toothed Shrews on the Isles of Scilly also eat large numbers of amphipod crustaceans living amongst rocks on the seashore. Although small in size, Greater White-toothed Shrews are reported to catch and eat lizards and small rodents.

Despite their general and opportunist feeding habits, studies on captive shrews show that they do discriminate between different prey, showing preference for some and distaste for others. Millipedes are not generally favoured as food because of their acrid secretion and ants are rarely eaten. Some molluscs, such as the garden slug *(Arion hortensis)*, are not much liked because of the copious slime they produce. Slugs and snails are usually eaten only when the mucus has been rubbed off with the shrew's forefeet or wiped off against the ground. Similarly, discrimination between different woodlice is shown: Common Shrews find the small *Philoscia* is the most palatable, while the large *Armadillidium*, with its thick exoskeleton and ability to roll into a ball, is least preferred.

THEIR VORACIOUS APPETITES

Shrews are renowned for their voracious appetites. In order to survive, they have to feed regularly and often, usually every two to three hours throughout day and night. They also require large quantities of food, although this varies according to species and body weight. Water Shrews eat approximately half their body weight in food every 24 hours; Common Shrews require about 80 to 90 per cent of their body weight and the tiny Pygmy Shrew consumes 1¼ times its own weight daily. White-toothed shrews are physiologically rather different and, although much the same size as Common Shrews, they eat only about half their body weight daily on account of their slightly lower metabolic rates.

These estimates of food consumption tend to exaggerate the appetite of shrews since they fail to take into account the high water content of animal prey; most invertebrates comprise at least 70 per cent water. If the food consumption of a Common Shrew living on maggots is compared with a mouse of similar size feeding on dry seeds, they both eat similar amounts in terms of the dry weight equivalent of food eaten daily. Most invertebrates also have a large amount of indigestible chitinous exoskeleton.

Nevertheless, a Common Shrew has to find and eat about a hundred maggot-sized prey every 24 hours. How does it find sufficient prey to sustain it from day to day? The general and opportunist feeding habits of shrews allow them to eat almost any common and readily available invertebrate. These prey are extremely abundant amongst the vegetation, leaf litter and underlying soil and even in winter they number many hundreds per square metre, although locating them in freezing conditions may be difficult.

FORAGING BEHAVIOUR

Shrews spend most of their life foraging and are very efficient hunters, able to pursue running prey and locate those buried in the soil or hidden amongst vegetation. Captive Common Shrews, for example, can locate and dig out quiescent prey such as insect pupae buried up to 12 cm (4¾ inches) deep in soil. The shrew's

10 (left). *European Water Shrew showing typical bicoloured pelage.*

11 (right). *The Greater White-toothed Shrew: a big-eared shrew.*

12 (below). *White-toothed Shrew showing the typical shrew features of tiny eyes and a long, pointed snout well supplied with touch-sensitive whiskers.*

eyes are very small and vision is poor and of little use in locating prey but its olfactory ability is much better developed and shrews have sensitive snouts furnished with touch-sensitive whiskers or vibrissae. A combination of smell, touch and hearing and very thorough searching are used to find prey.

When out foraging, a shrew runs over the ground, pushing through the undergrowth and leaf litter, stopping at intervals to probe with the snout and dig with the forefeet. As soon as a prey item is located it is immobilised with bites to its head and is then eaten, usually from the head down. Unpalatable or highly chitinised parts of the prey such as legs or large wings may be discarded. Captive shrews sometimes cache surplus food in the nest or in a small depression in the ground which they cover with leaves, and it is probable that wild shrews do this when a clump of prey is discovered. The difference in size and physique between Common and Pygmy Shrews reflects a slight difference in foraging mode: the more robust Common Shrew hunts for subterranean prey, such as earthworms, as well as for prey on the ground surface, while the Pygmy Shrew is confined more to foraging amongst vegetation on the ground surface.

All shrews can swim but only Water Shrews hunt underwater. They dive to the bottom of a stream or pond and search among the stones and submerged plants with snout and forefeet, picking up any prey in the mouth and carrying it to the bank or a nearby rock before killing and eating it. Caddis larvae, some of their favourite prey, may have to be extracted from their stone or twig cases before they can be eaten. The shrew bites off the top of the case so that it can reach the head of

13. *Shrews are renowned for their ferocity. Here, a Lesser White-toothed Shrew demonstrates its bite.*

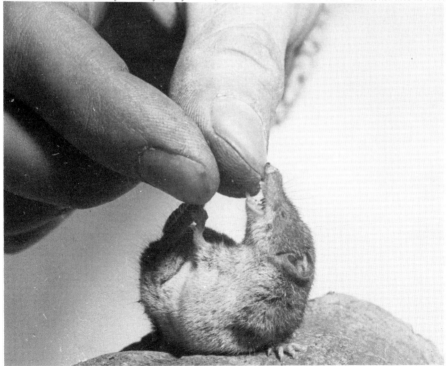

the larva and then pulls it free from its case. There is evidence that Water Shrews produce a toxic secretion in the saliva which probably helps to immobilise the prey, particularly amphibians, fish and larger invertebrates, by its effects on the nervous system. The bite of a Water Shrew can be quite painful to a human hand for, although shrews' teeth rarely puncture the skin, this toxin in the saliva seems to produce a slight inflammation and reddening of the skin at the site of the bite which persists for several days.

Water Shrews can dive to over 1 metre (3 feet) in depth but each dive lasts only a few seconds. They are very buoyant because of their rounded shape and the layer of air trapped by the dense fur, so they must paddle hard to stay underwater and may hold on to rocks or plants in order to remain submerged. They usually hunt in shallow water around 30 cm (1 foot) deep, where it is easier for them to reach freshwater shrimps and other such prey living amongst the substratum. Shallow water, the abundance of suitable prey and the clean conditions may be the reasons why watercress beds are so popular with Water Shrews.

Many dives are unsuccessful and no prey is caught. It is also common for Water Shrews to confuse pieces of twig, plant stems, small stones and empty caddis larvae cases for live prey while foraging underwater. Only when the shrew returns to land with the object is it discarded. Water Shrews usually have favourite landing and feeding places where it is often possible to find these discarded objects together with tell-tale remains of invertebrates such as caddis cases and snail shells. So foraging underwater may be energetically costly and quite inefficient but it does reduce competition with other species of shrew.

Shrews sometimes indulge in an activity known as refection which resembles the habit of coprophagy in rabbits and which may have a similar function of extracting further nutrients from the food. A shrew will curl up on its side or back, usually when in its nest, and spend a minute or so licking up a milky white fluid from the everted rectum, but it does not appear to eat the faeces.

Activity and rest

Most shrews must feed regularly every two hours or so or they will die of starvation, so they must be active both by day and by night. Their active periods are spent bustling swiftly through the undergrowth in the relentless search for food. They have bouts of activity spent foraging and exploring which last from about thirty minutes to two hours, and these alternate with periods of rest of similar length which are spent in the nest. Their nests are rounded in shape and constructed of dried grass, leaves, moss and even small stones and they have several entrances. Complete rest lasts only a few minutes at a time and is interrupted by periods of nest repair, feeding on cached prey and, sometimes, grooming.

Grooming consists merely of vigorous scratching of the fur with the hind feet and rarely of licking. This seems to be sufficient to keep the short fur in good order, for wild shrews always look extremely shiny and healthy. Water Shrews, however, indulge in much more careful grooming, particularly after diving. Although their fur is more water-repellent than that of the strictly terrestrial shrews, it does become wet with successive dives and the surplus is removed by frequent scratching and shaking. Squeezing the body through their narrow burrows also seems to help remove excess water from the fur. It is most important that these shrews do not get wet and chilled.

A period of intense activity may be interrupted suddenly by the need for a rest but, instead of returning to the nest, a shrew may have a short nap wherever it happens to be. It remains motionless for a few seconds with head and nose tucked up against the chest and then it wakes and resumes its activities.

Both Common and Water Shrews are most active during the night and at dawn and dusk. They are least active around midday and early afternoon. Pygmy Shrews have a similar pattern of activity but are equally active by day and by night

14. *Baby Common Shrew eight days after birth.*

15. *A nest of young Common Shrews twelve days old with the mother in attendance.*

16. Albino individuals occasionally occur. This one is a North American Short-tailed Shrew.

and each alternating active and resting period tends to be shorter than in Common Shrews. White-toothed shrews are generally slower and less agile in their movements and reactions and are less active than Common and Pygmy Shrews, possibly as a result of their lower metabolic rates.

Shrews must remain active throughout the winter and in all weathers. They cannot hibernate because they are too small to store sufficient quantities of fat to sustain them during long periods of inactivity. However, they are less active above ground in cold weather and spend longer periods in the nest and probably in underground tunnel systems where they forage. White-toothed shrews can be induced to reduce their metabolism and become quite torpid in captivity, but not so the other species. Pygmy Shrews spend relatively more of their time above ground compared with Common Shrews.

Breeding

FINDING A MATE

Shrews in northern temperate regions generally mature in the spring (March and April) following their birth in the previous summer and are then ready to breed. Males mature slightly earlier than females. The sexes are very difficult to tell apart while the shrews are immature, but once they have developed into breeding condition the females are distinguishable by the three pairs of abdominal nipples (five pairs in the case of the Water Shrew) and the male by prominent bulges occupied by the testes on either side of the abdomen near the tail. The males roam widely in search of females but attempts to mate are frequently met with fierce rebuffs accompanied by loud squeaking and scuffling. Only when the female is in oestrus is she receptive to the male's advances and willing to mate with him. This period of oestrus lasts only some 24 hours at a time every three weeks or so in the reproductive cycle of the female. Courtship is minimal and mating is brief. The male mounts the female and uses his teeth to hold her by the nape of the neck or the top of the head and this may create a small, bare patch there. Mated females can often be identified by this means. The male shows no further interest in his partner after mating and wanders off in search of other females, contributing nothing to the rearing of the young.

BIRTH AND DEVELOPMENT OF THE YOUNG

The young shrews are born between May and September after a gestation period of about 22 days. The female constructs a large domed nest of leaves and dried grass beneath a log, in a grass tussock or in an underground burrow. Here she gives birth to between three and nine blind hairless young, of which several will die in infancy. At birth young Common Shrews weigh about 0.5 gram and Pygmy Shrews about 0.25 gram, but the young grow very rapidly and within a week or so are able to crawl around the nest. If they are dislodged from the nest, they utter loud distress calls which attract the mother, who hurries to find them. She carries them back to the nest in her mouth or drags them by the scruff of the neck.

The fur of young Common Shrews first appears as a grey down at about nine days after birth, and by eleven days the teeth show their characteristic red tips. By fourteen days of age the young look like real shrews: they already weigh 5 to 7 grams, are covered in short, fine, greyish fur and their eyes are beginning to open. At this time of rapid growth of the young, the nursing mother's food intake increases to about 120 per cent of her body weight per day.

By sixteen days of age the eyes are fully open and the young ones then begin to venture out of the nest for short periods. At this time they may follow their mother in a 'caravan'. Although characteristic of white-toothed shrews, this habit has been observed in Common Shrews and may be associated with disturbance of the nest. Each young shrew grasps the base of the tail of the preceding shrew so that the mother runs along with the young trailing in a line behind her. In this way they can be led directly to a new nest. Caravanning may also be used to encourage exploration and extend the young shrews' knowledge of the environment outside the nest.

At about 21 days old the young begin to catch and eat live invertebrate prey, but they still attempt to get milk from their mother.

The young shrews are fully weaned and are nearly fully grown at 22 to 25 days of age, and they are encouraged to leave the nest when the mother becomes increasingly intolerant of them. The young also indulge in threat calls and scuffles with each other and within a few days of weaning they disperse to find their own nesting sites and are fully independent.

White-toothed shrews have smaller litters than Common Shrews, with an average of 3 to 4 young, and the young are slightly larger and better developed at birth, weighing nearly 1 gram. Consequently their development is more rapid and their eyes are open and pelage fully grown by a mere nine days after birth.

The breeding season lasts from April to September but has a peak in July and August. A female shrew may produce two or possibly three litters during the course of a summer.

The shrew's year

POPULATION CYCLES AND SURVIVAL RATES

Shrew populations reach their peak in summer when breeding occurs. Although adults and young are similar in size, the juveniles can be distinguished from the parent generation by their hairier tails and unworn teeth. Population sizes generally decline in autumn and remain at a low level through the winter before breeding commences in the following spring. These seasonal cycles differ in magnitude from year to year depending upon the climate and other environmental factors.

There is a rapid die-off of shrews in autumn. By this time the old adults have finished breeding and they die, largely as a result of the effects of old age, such as worn teeth and an inability to compete with younger, fitter animals and to avoid predation. A shrew's teeth do not grow throughout life and so experience considerable wear, even after a mere nine to twelve months of life. There is also very high mortality of inexperienced juveniles in summer and autumn as they disperse from their place of birth and establish new home ranges and search for suitable nest sites. Some 50 per cent of Common Shrews disappear in this way within the first two months of life, probably as a result of predation.

In winter, shrews are rarely seen or heard and it is often assumed that they either hibernate or die, but they do remain active through the winter and survive surprisingly well. Their mortality rate is actually lower in winter than at other times of year, although only about 20 to 30 per cent of the animals born in the previous summer will survive to breed in the ensuing spring.

LONGEVITY

Shrews are very short-lived: in the wild, few Common Shrews reach the extreme old age of twelve months, and Pygmy Shrews have a similar lifespan. Water Shrews may live up to nineteen months in the wild. White-toothed shrews have a slightly longer lifespan than the other species: Greater White-toothed shrews have been known to survive for eighteen months in the wild. All shrews can live longer in captivity and a Greater White-toothed Shrew survived for a record period of four years.

Generally the adults of most species of shrew die after breeding and the young then carry the population through the winter and into the following spring, when it will be their turn to breed.

PREDATORS

By far the most important predators of shrews are tawny owls and barn owls. Common Shrews constitute between 5 and 13 per cent by weight of the diet of tawny owls. Kestrels, stoats, weasels and foxes are known to take shrews, but much less frequently. The dispersing juveniles are particularly vulnerable to predation. Domestic cats often catch and kill shrews but do not eat them. Shrews are unpalatable to many predators, including cats, because of the musky odour they produce. However, this musky scent is unlikely to provide much protection from predators since cats, for example, do not learn to avoid catching shrews because they are distasteful to eat.

PARASITES

Shrews are hosts for a wide variety of parasites, both internally and externally. Internally, shrews harbour numbers of different digenean flukes, tapeworms and nematodes in the stomach and gut. This high diversity and density of internal parasites results from the shrew's feeding habits. Many of their prey, particularly beetles, slugs and snails, act as intermediate hosts of these parasites, which are transmitted as the shrew feeds. The parasite load varies with the age of the shrew and the season. Shrews accumulate internal parasites as they age and an old shrew in midsummer may harbour over twenty tapeworms living in its gut. A very common parasite is the nematode worm *Porrocaecum talpae,* which lies coiled up under the skin of shrews. Its final host is an owl, which takes in the parasite by eating infected shrews.

Externally, shrews carry fleas, mites and ticks. The fleas are large and brown and easily visible amongst the fur. Despite a shrew's small size, it may carry several fleas at the same time, especially in summer when the population numbers of both shrews and parasites are high. Mites are very common on the skin and amongst the dense fur but are very small and not easily seen.

While these various parasites may be a source of irritation to the shrew they are not a major cause of mortality and they are not generally transmissible to man.

MOULTING

In autumn and winter shrews in northern temperate regions undergo moulting. The Common Shrew, for example,

17. Owls are the major predators of shrews. Here, a barn owl has caught a Common Shrew.

moults in September and October and replaces its juvenile pelage of short summer hairs, only about 2 mm in length, with a thick winter coat which is darker in colour and consists of hairs some 6 mm in length. This moult commences at the rump of the shrew and then progresses forwards to the head. In the spring, between March and May, two moults occur in quick succession but these proceed in the opposite direction, starting at the head. The thick winter coat is dispensed with and is replaced by a sleek summer coat. Pygmy Shrews moult in much the same way but, strangely, the moults proceed in the opposite directions to those of the Common Shrew.

SEASONAL WEIGHT CHANGES

Many shrews in temperate regions, including Common, Pygmy and Water Shrews, undergo seasonal changes in body weight with a marked decrease during winter. Young Common Shrews born during the summer achieve weights of 7 to 8 grams by September or October but, as winter approaches, they decrease in weight to as little as 5.5 grams, incurring a weight loss in the order of 27 per cent in Britain. Their body weights reach a minimum between December and February and then a great spurt of growth occurs in March and April as they put on weight and become sexually mature, and by summer they weigh 10 to 12 grams.

The phenomenon of the winter weight loss is not, however, found in the white-toothed shrews.

Wild shrews seem unable to store up fat in any quantity: it seems that they have such an active life that they never get fat. Consequently these seasonal weight changes are not due to cycles of fat storage. The winter weight decrease has yet to be fully accounted for but it is largely brought about by changes in dimension of the skeleton, notably the cranium, and of certain internal organs such as the adrenal bodies, as well as a reduction in body protein and water content.

It is commonly assumed that the weight loss is the result of reduced food supply in cold, winter conditions but this is unlikely since food supply is not depleted in winter, although it may be less accessible in frosty conditions. Temperature and day length may provide cues for changes in body weight but the exact cause has yet to be explained.

It is suggested that the loss of weight may be a strategy to reduce food requirements in winter. A small animal eats less food than a large animal and so would need to devote less time to foraging in cold, winter conditions and could thus conserve energy. To a Common Shrew this could make a difference of about twenty maggot-sized prey and up to five hours of foraging time per day.

Social organisation

SPATIAL ORGANISATION

Shrews are essentially solitary animals and each maintains its own home range, to which it confines its activities. Here it nests, forages and explores. This area may well be a territory which is actively defended against intruders, but evidence of this is conflicting. The home ranges of different individuals frequently overlap, at least in part, especially during the breeding season when males are moving around in search of females. However, there is evidence to suggest that their home ranges may be mutually exclusive, particularly in winter, and captive Common Shrews will chase others away from their own adopted home area. Even the presence of a stuffed skin of a shrew will elicit a violent reaction from the territory owner. The skin will be repeatedly attacked and bitten until it is torn apart. If two Common Shrews are caught alive in the same trap, one will invariably kill and eat the other.

Both male and female Common Shrews maintain home ranges of similar sizes. These home ranges are often smaller in winter than in summer but generally they occupy areas of 370 to 630 square metres (4000 to 6800 square feet), occasionally up to 1000 square metres (10,800 square feet). As a young shrew becomes independent from its mother it searches for and then adopts a suitable area as its home range. Once established, this home range will remain in much the same location throughout the life of a shrew. Common Shrews can be found in the same small area month after month from youth through to old age. However, in the breeding season wandering males may travel over 100 metres (110 yards) from their normal home-range area in search of mates.

Pygmy Shrews resemble Common Shrews in their spatial organisation but, despite their smaller size, they have larger home ranges than Common Shrews, occupying 500 to 1800 square metres (5400 to 19,400 square feet). Even in Ireland, where there are no other species of shrew to compete for space and resources, Pygmy Shrews maintain these large home ranges.

Water Shrews often live in quite close proximity to each other and so their home ranges usually overlap. Several Water Shrews may inhabit the same burrow system. They occupy some 30 to 80 metres (33 to 87 yards) along the banks of streams or rivers as well as an adjacent area of water. Little is known about their ranging behaviour for they seem to spend only a brief time, perhaps a few months, in one area and then pass on. So, unlike the stay-at-home Common Shrew, the Water Shrew has frequent shifts of home range.

White-toothed shrews also have overlapping home ranges. Males of the Lesser White-toothed Shrew have home ranges of 50 metres (55 yards) or less in diameter while those of females are considerably smaller.

SOCIAL BEHAVIOUR AND COMMUNICATION

Shrews are generally solitary and unsociable and so tend to avoid direct contact with each other. To advertise their presence and help them avoid one another, scent marking may be employed. Shrews produce a characteristic musky smell, much of which derives from a gland on each flank between the fore and hind legs. In Common and Pygmy Shrews, for example, these lateral flank glands are small, oval areas of skin rich in blood vessels and containing many sebaceous and sweat glands, and bordered by short, stiff hairs. When fully grown they produce a highly odoriferous and rather greasy secretion which sticks to the overlying fur and rubs off on to the vegetation and the walls of burrows as the shrew passes by. The scent is quite long-lived, persisting for several days. Its function may be to mark out a territory and discourage strangers but evidence for its use is conflicting since not all age classes of shrews possess active flank glands. The glands are only poorly developed in juveniles and appear to have no function during winter when it would seem most advantageous to be able to advertise ownership of territories, but they develop in both sexes as the shrews age. They show maximum development in mature males and may be associated not only with marking out territories but also with advertising breeding condition. Those of adult females are clearly visible but not so active in their secretion, possibly in order that males are not discouraged from entering their territories to mate with them. Their precise role has yet to be determined.

The white-toothed shrews are much more smelly than Common and Pygmy Shrews and are often known as musk shrews. Their characteristic sweet, musky odour is very persistent and can be detected on the hands following handling of these shrews, even after several washes. Lesser White-toothed Shrews have been seen to 'belly-mark' both in their own home ranges and in unfamiliar places in captivity. With the hind feet spread, the belly is pressed to the ground and the body dragged forward by the forefeet, rubbing the lateral flank glands and the anal area against the ground. 'Chinning' has occasionally been observed too: the underside of the chin is rubbed against prominent objects in a manner similar to that of rabbits. This behaviour has not been seen in other shrews, though.

Scent is also deposited with the faeces and scent marking may occur by strategic placing of the droppings around the borders of a territory or home range or in other prominent places. Captive shrews usually deposit their droppings in faecal middens in the far corners of their cages or enclosures.

Shrews communicate more directly by means of calls. Common Shrews are particularly vocal and a range of calls is employed, but the most obvious to human ears is the succession of piercing, staccato squeaks or shrieks of warning which are produced when a shrew is angry or alarmed. At close quarters, these shrieks may be replaced by lower-pitched, rolling churls. When two shrews meet they momentarily freeze and then commence loud squeaking as they face each other. With heads up, mouths open and snouts contracted, each vocalises loudly to warn off the other. This vocal sparring may be enough to discourage further social intercourse and one of the shrews will retreat.

However, Common and Pygmy Shrews are very pugnacious and vocalisation my give rise to scuffles. At first, they sit up on their hind legs and hit out with the forefeet. They then aim bites at each other's heads, whereupon one may throw itself on its back while still squeaking and kicking, and the other then runs off through the undergrowth. If neither shrew gives way they may become locked in combat before one breaks loose and retreats. Another sign of excitement or annoyance is the lashing of the tail rapidly from side to side. This is often done when wild shrews are handled.

Other vocalisations produced include the soft but high-pitched twitters which are emitted by Common Shrews as they explore and forage. Similar sounds are used between the female and her young in the nest. When distressed, the young will also produce loud squeaks resembling barks which immediately attract the attention of the mother.

Some of the sounds produced by shrews, particularly those of *Sorex* species, are ultrasonic in frequency. It has been suggested that these ultrasounds may be used in echo location, particularly when shrews are exploring new areas. If so, this echo-locating ability could function only crudely and over a short range and would not enable the location of prey in the cluttered habitat of plant roots and stems, leaf litter, stones and logs in which shrews live.

Not all species of shrew are equally aggressive. White-toothed shrews are more sociable than other species and individuals may share the same nest, even if of the same sex, and small groups can be kept together quite amicably in captivity. Greater White-toothed Shrews will form pairs during the breeding season in captivity and show aggression towards other individuals. The female will even tolerate the presence of the adult male in the nest with the young and will leave him with them while she goes out foraging. The male shows a tendency to shelter the young in the nest by crouching over them.

Water Shrews may also live in quite close proximity to their neighbours but they do not share nests. Interactions between individuals of this species are largely confined to loud calls as a protest against intruding neighbours, and scuffles ensue only if the intruder gets too close.

Different species of shrew frequently live in the same area, for example, Common and Pygmy Shrews usually share the same habitat. However, they seem to ignore each other and avoid direct contact.

Shrews and man

Shrews were the source of many superstitions in the past. The Romans believed that shrews were evil and throughout history they have been thought of as poisonous and even deadly. They were thought to cause lameness if they walked

18. *Common Shrew*

over sleeping cattle, and the mere presence of shrews in pastures was believed to cause the death of cattle and horses grazing there. Their pugnacious and apparently bad-tempered nature has not gone unnoticed and hence the description of the shrewish character in literature.

All these superstitions are unfounded. Far from being an evil influence, shrews are beneficial to man, largely as a result of their predatory habits and their voracious appetites. Many of the invertebrates upon which they feed are potential pests, such as cranefly larvae (leatherjackets), caterpillars and slugs, which are eaten in large numbers. Unlike many rodents, shrews rarely destroy seeds, bulbs or stored products, neither do they create piles of earth on lawns like moles do.

Many shrews have become accustomed to living in and around human habitations. These include the white-toothed shrews as already mentioned, and also the Large Musk Shrew, *Suncus murinus*, which has been repeatedly introduced by man to a variety of locations as far flung as Madagascar, Guam and New Guinea, probably accidentally in a similar manner to rats and mice. Although it sometimes damages stored products and is smelly and apparently noisy as a result of the incessant shrill chattering sounds it emits as it goes about its activities, it does destroy many pest insects and possibly even rodents. In China this shrew is known as the 'money shrew' because its chatterings are thought to resemble the jingling of coins.

Shrews also act as indicators of pesticides, pollutants and habitat change: being predators, they accumulate and concentrate chemicals in their bodies by feeding on invertebrates. Although they are ubiquitous, they do require some vegetation cover amongst which to live. They are therefore vulnerable to changing agricultural and industrial practices. Water Shrews are particularly vulnerable to the destruction of their aquatic habitats through pollution and drainage.

Shrews are easy to catch alive in pitfall traps and small mammal traps such as Longworth live-traps but they quickly die of starvation, cold and stress if not attended to promptly. They can be maintained quite easily in captivity provided they are given dry nesting material and abundant food such as maggots, mealworms or other live prey as well as chopped heart and eggs.

All species of shrews in Britain are now protected by law (Wildlife and Countryside Act, 1981) and it is an offence to kill a shrew without a special licence.

The habits of many species of shrew have never been studied in detail and some species are known only from a handful of specimens collected and lodged in museums. So there is still a lot to learn about these fascinating little mammals.

Useful information

FURTHER READING
Corbet, G. B., and Southern, H. N. (editors). *The Handbook of British Mammals.* Blackwell Scientific Publications, 1977.
Crowcroft, W. P. *The Life of the Shrew.* Max Reinhardt, 1957.
The Mammal Society, Baltic Exchange Buildings, 21 Bury Street, London EC3A 5AU. It welcomes all those interested in the study of mammals, both professional and amateur, young and old, and provides information about all mammal matters. Meetings are organised and members receive regular newsletters and can participate in surveys and other activities. A Youth Group caters for younger members.

ACKNOWLEDGEMENTS
All photographs are by David Hosking. Figure 1 is by Graham Allen and figures 5 and 9 by the author.